NOT JUST A TEACHER

THE MAKING OF A HIGHLY SUCCESSFUL TEACHER

I.U.THADDEUS

THE MAKING OF A HIGHLY SUCCESSFUL TEACHER

Printed in USA by CreateSpace

ISBN-13:
978-1545276433

ISBN-10:
1545276439

Website: www.equipux.com

Copyright 2017 I.U.Thaddeus

All Right Reserved
No part of this publication may be reproduced, stored in a retrieval system or transmitted, in any form or by any means, electronic, mechanical, photocopying, recording or otherwise without the prior permission of the author.

^^^

NOT JUST A TEACHER

DEDICATION

To the Almighty God - the source of my inspiration.

ACKNOWLEDGEMENT

Kudos to all the teachers around the world.

NOT JUST A TEACHER

It's Starts With A Little Psychology

If you are working your way through teacher's training college, you are getting a lot of great education that will give you the knowledge and the skills to teach young minds in the not too distant future. But you may not entirely know what kind of minor to declare or what kind of classes to take that will harmonize well with your concentration on becoming an educator.

One suggestion that would help you tremendously would be for you to add a concentration in psychology. Psychology is a field of study that can give you invaluable resources and abilities to manage a classroom full of students that otherwise might not be available to you. The reason psychology would help you so much is that when it gets right down to it, teaching and learning are very human events. And you don't just teach the mind. You teach the heart and the soul of the student as well. So by learning how the minds of your students "tick", you give yourself yet another advantage in you quest to maintain control of that classroom at all times.

When you are teaching a group of students, even if not a word is being said, they are talking to you all the time. And part of psychology is learning what they are saying to you with their body language. In general, students will send a signal of blocking you or being open to you based on how their arms are positioned, how relaxed they seem, whether their legs are crossed or open and particularly through their facial expression. If you can learn to understand the language of body language, you can use it to take a boring lesson or lecture and suddenly transform it into a lesson that captures the student's imagination and holds them for as long as you need to for the sake of the lesson.

    Psychology will also help you understand how to use your body language to send messages to your students. The thing about body language is that it delivers the message whether the other person is aware of it or not. You no doubt know that standing in front of a group of kids and teaching is about a lot more than what you say or even how you say it with your voice. You are communicating all the time with your body language, your posture and your movements. And if you know a little bit about human psychology and how your students will react to movement or sudden changes in your physical demeanor, you can use the power you have over them to capture their minds and hold them on the subject at hand. In that way psychology can be a powerful aid to your teaching.

Now you are not looking to become Sigmund Freud in your study of psychology. But if you know enough about the human mind and how what is going on inside a student can be expressed externally, you can be a big help to a student who may be in emotional trouble but unable to communicate it. If you can spot the signs of emotional distress and get that child to counseling and the help he or she needs, you could literally be a lifesaver for one of your students. And that is a wonderful feeling and all the reason you need to make psychology part of your college curriculum plan.

∧∧∧

A Modern Way to Start Your Career in Teaching

Not everybody goes into teaching by getting a degree right out of high school and making it a profession from there on out. Many wonderful teachers take on the profession as a second career. There are a lot of reasons it happens like that. Perhaps you are unhappy in your current career but you keep doing a certain job because it pays the bills. It is very easy in youth to just fall into a job niche because it happened to be a job you got, then after you developed a resume and got additional training, you found it difficult to leave that job to pursue your passion.

Teaching is as much a calling as it is a profession. As a profession, it's often a career that does not attract the best and the brightest to become teachers because the pay is low and the frustrations and demands are high. So many people who may at heart be "born teachers" spend some of their adult life in other professions. If this is your story, you may be coming to a place in your life when that inner teacher is struggling to get out and get you into the career you of teaching young people full time.

The good news is that in this modern time, much progress has been made to offer you a way to get the degree, the education and the certification to make that transition from your current career to a life of a teacher with little disruption to your life. One such way is to get your teaching degree from an online university as a remote student, in that way, you step through all of the requirements for your degree using the internet and eventually get that degree so you can easily transition into a life of a full time teacher.

It used to be considered farfetched to get an entire degree online. But almost every university in the world now offers a remote study program so you can satisfy every aspect of a degree plan on your own schedule using the internet as your classroom and your teacher. The lectures can be presented as video files and you can even participate in group projects and discussions via chat, message boards and wikis that the lecturer can set up to bring you along through each class.

The good of this kind of program is that you can go about getting your teaching degree while continuing to hold down your full time job. Because the "classes" you take are online and recorded, except for live events such as team meetings, you can take each session when you get home from work and even pause them to deal with family issues and then continue when things quite down. This is an ideal situation for adult education when quitting your job to get another degree is just not practical.

The hard part about getting your degree online is that, like study by mail programs, the discipline to keep up, to "attend" class and to do your reading and homework is entirely put on you to stay with. It's very easy for life's demands to draw you away from your degree plan and to slow or stop you which then make getting the momentum going even more difficult.

∧∧∧

NOT JUST A TEACHER

But if you enlist the aid of your family and establish times when dad or mom are "in class" even if you are just locked in your study doing your online coursework, that regimen can help you get through your classes and successfully graduate ready to start a career in teaching. And when you are finally doing the job you feel is your calling to do teaching youth, the hard work of taking that degree from an online program will pay off.

Becoming a Truly Professional Teacher

There is something so satisfying about working with a true professional in any line of work. When you have a professional on the job in any area of specialization watching that person in action is like watching a work of art. They exude the knowledge, the skill, the devotion to doing a top notch job and the confidence that they are the professional who can do the job that is missing in a lesser talent.

That is the level we all want to reach in the field of teaching if that is your calling. Not only do you want to be a true professional in your area of specialization which is teaching, you want your students to notice your professionalism and recognize that it makes a big difference having a professional running the class rather an a lesser talent.

^^^

NOT JUST A TEACHER

When a professional is on the case, everybody relaxes because they know the job will be done right. In the movie, Pulp Fiction, when the gangsters needed help because of a killing, they called in Mr. Wolf. And Mr. Wolf was well known for being the man that always knows what to do, who moves fast but is as courteous as he is efficient and who knows how to get the job done right. When Mr. Wolf was on the scene, the problem was as good as solved. And even though that movie was a bit grisly and profane, Mr. Wolf is a great example of true professionalism at work.

So how do you show your professionalism as you go about your craft of teaching? For one thing, you dress the part. Take pride in your wardrobe and present to yourself to your class each day in a garment that says, I came ready to teach so you should come ready to learn. That is what happens when a professional is on the premises. Everybody wants to get on board with the program.

A professional always knows what to do both long range and right now. That means you come prepared. Your lesson plans are in order, your room is prepared and you paperwork is organized so at no time do you have to pause and get yourself together when you are into the process of teaching your students. This will take some time for you to get to that level of organization when you walk in the door of your classroom the next day. But putting in that hour or two each night so you are that organized not only makes you a better teacher, it lets the students know that this is a professional operation so be ready.

Students, particularly youth and children can tell the difference

^^^

between someone who knows what they are doing and someone who is floundering. As the saying goes, "they can smell fear." It gives young people confidence and a sense of security that you are organized and not only know what you are going to do each moment of the teaching day, you know what they are going to do as well. That is professionalism and it will make a world of difference in how your teaching goes.

    A professional teacher also responds to interruptions and even disturbances calmly because you have seen it before and you know what to do. Of course developing a history in teaching to where you really do know what to do in each circumstance takes time. But if you are completely prepared in every other respect, interruptions won't throw you because you can address them and be right back to you lesson smoothly and calmly.

A byproduct of being consummately prepared and so well versed in what your lesson plans say and what you are teaching is that it gives you a calm confidence that frees you up to be relaxed and even humorous with your students. When your students see you smile because everything is going exactly the way you want it to go, they will respond and open up to you because they sense your confidence and they want to see where you are going to take them. And because you are relaxed and at ease, your students are at ease as well and they can ask you questions and interact with you as you teach. And that kind of interactive dialog is what makes the difference in the lives of students and makes you a true professional teacher.

∧∧∧

Breaking into the Working World of Teachers

In every training college in the world, there are ambitious and starry eyed youngsters who are preparing for a career in teaching. At some point that army of graduates will hit the streets to find jobs in the field of teaching. What is not often taught in colleges are the real world skills of how to actually find and land a good teaching job right out of school. And while there is always a need for good teachers, the new graduate should develop some skills in finding the kind of teaching job that they always dreamed of so even from that first engagement, their career in teaching gets off on the right foot.

There is a lot you can do even before graduation day to get your job search moving and to make yourself desirable as a teacher so when school administrators get flooded with applications from newly graduated teachers, you stand out as the one they want to call in for an interview. One thing you can do at any time during you academic career is to intern as a teaching assistant and volunteer to teach in underprivileged schools.

You can teach just a few hours a day and work it around your academic work. By taking on the working world of teaching even before you have your degree, you will be able to present yourself to employers post graduation as someone who has real world experience in the classroom and "knows the ropes" of getting through an academic year with real live students. That is tremendously valuable to a school administrator with a spot to fill because it reduces the concern that a new graduate who

∧∧∧

has never faced a classroom full of restless children might wash out when the reality of what teaching is really like.

Another way to get a jump start on the market before students flood the schools for jobs is to start your search early in your last semester of school. Schools know by February or March if they will have jobs to fill for the next academic year. So if you begin your search for a teaching position in March or April, you can often land an interview or even secure a position for the fall long before many of your contemporaries in school begin their hunt for their first teaching job.

Becoming proactive like this always gives you the advantage in finding the job you really want rather than just "any job" in the teaching profession. Spend some time narrowing down exactly what kind of teaching position you want and at what level you feel your personality and teaching style will benefit students the most. You may do much better with young children than with teenagers or you may wish to focus on high scholars because they are more intellectually equipped to grasp the subject matter with you. By knowing well in advance where you want to teach, you can target those kinds of positions in your job search and improve your chances of finding that perfect teaching job.

You should make the phrase "leave no stone unturned" your motto for hunting up the teaching jobs that are open in your community. First of all, be very proactive in your search. Just because you are graduating, even with honors, with your teaching degree, that doesn't mean the schools will seek you out with jobs. So you take the search to them before someone else does. And in doing so it will be you that gets the premium teaching positions rather than have to take "what's left" after the good teaching positions are snatched up by more aggressive graduates.

There are lots of ways you can flush out those teaching jobs. Check the Human Resource or Employment offices at the schools you would like to be a part of and keep an eye on their employment notice boards. Use the internet wisely, watch the newspaper and even get in touch with placement agencies that are known for placing new teachers.

But above all, network, network, network. Use every contact you have and forge new relationships to get the inside scoop on jobs before they even become public. Networking is the number one best way to find great teaching positions so you should use it extensively to find a position to get your teaching career off on a great start toward a great future of success in the field of teaching.

∧∧∧

Decorum in Teaching

One reason that many if not most teachers go into teaching in the first place is that you have a love of children or of youth and you not only love teaching them but you love hanging around with them. Teachers are very often driven by an inner passion for their students and for the subject matter that is their primary reason for showing up to teach the children of others in the first place. It takes that kind of passion to overcome the many obstacles, difficulties and roadblocks that are thrown in the way of the teaching process not to mention the low pay.

As a result teachers as a rule tend to be people driven more by passion and values than by money or even career advancement. Teaching is a profession where you will see a teacher work for decades just teaching algebra to a particular class and never moving on. He or she is not stuck at that job level. That is just the nature of the teaching profession because teachers at heart are driven to teach.

But it is important to know about decorum in teaching as well. You enjoy your students and that warm relationship between teacher and student creates the chemistry that makes class time work so well. But there are limits to how much you can show your affection and areas you need to be aware of to avoid any appearance of impropriety between teacher and student. Some rules of behavior that must become as much a part of how you tick as your lesson plans and grading system are…

∧∧∧

- Limit your expressions of friendliness to smiles and supportive statements about the student academically. Never compliment how a student looks or imply that you like or love a student even though the act of teaching does generate warm relationships and emotions about your kids.

- If at all possible, never touch a student. This is a difficult rule to follow because the very act of being in the same classroom with 20-30 students for hours at a time makes physical contact hard to avoid. But limit intentional contact especially if it is to show affection. It can be misinterpreted way too easily.

➢ Watch your eyes, especially male teachers and especially in the junior and senior school grade levels. Students are very aware of the physical picture they present to the world. It is especially difficult to mind this rule when the girls in your class dress in a way that draws the eye even if you mean nothing by it. You have to develop almost a physical discipline to focus your eyes on the faces of the students you teach because even if you are thinking of something else entirely and your eyes rest somewhere that might be misunderstood, that can lead to trouble.

➢ Never be alone with a student of either gender. This is even more for your protection than it is for the protection of the student.

Many of these kind of decorum rules are to avoid the possibility of being falsely accused of some form of inappropriate behavior. Sadly because there has been widely publicized inappropriate behavior between students and teachers, good teachers everywhere have had to learn to live in this austere way because overzealous parents, fellow teachers, volunteers or even students can see something and decide to make an issue of it. And once something like that gets started, it is very difficult to stop.

∧∧∧

How Long Can You Teach?

If you are just preparing to enter the ranks of professional teachers and you are not a recent college graduate, it's easy to feel a bit insecure and ask that question, "Can you teach if you are old?" It's a fair question even if you are not so far along in life that you consider yourself to be "old". But it is easy to feel old if you are a middle aged or senior adult among 20 year olds in teacher college and if the competition for the teaching jobs are kids that could be your own sons or daughters.

There are a lot of jobs where there is a noticeable age bias against older workers. In the business world, sometimes companies prefer to hire younger workers because they work cheap and if they work out, there is such a longer career life ahead of them. But even in the business setting, many forward thinking employers are beginning to realize that the ranks of older workers contain a group of workers who are stable, hard working and devoted employees. So too schools are realizing more and more that hiring an older worker is not a disadvantage at all but that you bring a lot of good with you that the school should be thrilled to have.

If anything the profession of teaching is a perfect environment for someone who has seen a bit of life and who has matured and perhaps raised children of their own. Teaching full time while rewarding can be a huge challenge because it is sometimes hard to establish your authority in the class room and there are so many ways for a disruption to hurt the flow of teaching that is so important to accomplish your academic goals each day. An older worker is less prone to panic about disruptions or sudden problems that might come up as you teach and you have the experience and maturity to handle the problem efficiently without upsetting the rest of the class and get everyone back on task quickly.

It could be that one concern those who hire new teachers might have with an older worker is energy. Younger workers are able to keep up physically with children and they need to know that you won't tire during a long school day and that you have the physical stamina to get through a school day and come back for more tomorrow. There are a number of ways you can demonstrate that you are in shape and up to the challenge of teaching. You can put on a show of energy and enthusiasm during the interview. Or you could go so far as to offer to substitute teach or be a teacher assistant for a day so the administrator can witness first hand our energy and ability to "keep up" with those kiddos.

There is a good chance that not only will you encounter no age based bias or discrimination from school administrators, you will find that they already have a number of older teachers on staff so they know the value the school gets from that experience and wisdom. But the relationship that may give you more concern is whether the students can accept an older teacher and give you the same respect and regard that they would give to someone just out of college.

It may come as the biggest surprise of them all that children and even teenagers really do not mind older teachers or older people for that matter. After all, to a child, every

^^^

adult is an older teacher so they may not even notice that you are 20 years older than their last teacher. To a kid, old is old so what's the difference? Moreover, children have relationships with parents, uncles and aunts and grandparents that are loving and respectful so if they lump you in with those role models, you have it made.

What students don't like are older people who try to deny that they are old, who are ashamed of their age or who try to act younger than they are. Youth crave honesty. And youth are also quite aware that older age awaits them down the road so the last thing they want to see is you showing shame or discomfort because of your age. By being honest about your age with the kids, they will embrace you easily and you will have no difficulty teaching them.

ᴧᴧᴧ

Giving Your Students an Appreciation of the Arts

When you set out to become a teacher, it isn't always enough just to teach a rote set of knowledge. You want to give your students an appreciation for the each knowledge area so they not only know things and how to do things, they also understand the history behind the knowledge they have and have an ability to appreciate the nuances of what they have learned. There may be no area of learning that this concept applies to more than art.

By art, I mean the arts which may include music, vocal interpretation, creative writing and the visual arts. Now in many schools, art programs have gone by the wayside due to budget cuts. This is even more of a reason that if you want to learn to teach the arts to your students, you should come to the task with enthusiasm and some creative thinking so you can take advantage of this time when you can offer lessons in artistic development and appreciation.

Perhaps the biggest challenge of offering art classes as part of the curriculum at the school where you teach is to get kids who may not think they have artistic talent to take the course. In most cases art classes are not required but you still want to be able to touch as much as the student body as possible with an appreciation of the arts and give everyone a chance to take a stab at making a bit of art themselves.

Much of the work that will go into letting kids know it's ok to take art even if they do not feel they have artistic talent comes from the attitude of the teacher. Too often art teachers send the message that they expect every student to show noticeable artistic talent and that their grade may depend on their ability to produce art that can be judged as "good" by the teacher.

This creates huge stress in the students because nobody can just "become artistic." And sending that message defeats the purpose of offering a program in the arts to the students at your school in first place. But if you can encourage a spirit of play and exploration so that even students with no artistic talent at all are willing to take the class just to "give it a try", learning how art is made by making some of their own will be an enriching experience that may instill a love of art in the student that could last a lifetime.

In the movie The Music Man, the professor got two tone deaf children to sing "I love music mommy" as part of his effort to bring band music to a small town in Iowa. The pride those children and their parents showed more than offset that the song they offered to their portents was pretty unrecognizable as real music. But that scene is instructive in what you want to achieve in your students by giving them a chance to learn to create art with no regard for their talent one way or another. And don't be surprised if a student takes home a perfectly hideous artwork with pride and that piece of art becoming a precious heirloom for that family not because it is good art but because it is an expression of artistic feeling from a child who wanted to try something new and did it.

Along with giving our students the basic instructions in how to create works of art, don't miss out on the opportunity to give them a basic education in art history and art appreciation. This may be the greatest gift your art classes can give a child. If they come from your class with an awareness of why Michelangelo is one of the greatest artists of all time that is a part of our cultural knowledge that will demonstrate that this child has been given a broad and well rounded education.

Teaching art and art approbation can be one of the most fulfilling forms of teaching that you can offer to the next generation. Not only will the children have a lot of fun discovering the artists inside them, you will have a great time showing that side to them as well. And all of that fun will make them better people which, after all, is the goal of being an educator in the first place.

∧∧∧

Going to Bat for Your Students

When you set out to become a teacher, you set out to do more than just learn the skill of presenting information to a group of students. A teacher is much more than just someone who hands out information and then gives tests and grades. When you become a teacher, you become an entirely different kind of person. Becoming a teacher changes you or rather it allows that inner teacher to come to dominance and become what you were put here to be in the first place.

As just as being a teacher is a state of mind, teaching is about more than just giving lectures. One of the joys of teaching is the strong bond you develop with your students. When you take a small group of students through an entire school year of academics, you become a partner with them for their success. You become a confidant, a protector and a friend of the students and their families. This is a trusted place in the heart of your students and one that is not given lightly so cherish it and protect it at all costs.

One way that this bond is expressed is in how you will go to bat for a student if the need arises. That is because you can see beyond the outside view of what a kid is. You may have children in your class that have tattoos, earrings, wear gang colors or demonstrate violent behavior outside of class. But to you, that is a child who deserves to be loved, taught and cared for. It is not uncommon for this unique bond between teacher and student to turn a kid around and see him turn away from socially undesirable behavior and begin a long slow growth toward a productive lifestyle he learned from you, his teacher.

Going to bat for your student means that when you know a child is gifted, you use your influence with the administration to get that child the special educational opportunities that will develop that blessing in that child. If the gift is not in the area of broad educational excellence but in a specialized skill like music, art or athletics, you go to bat for that child to get him or her audition with the coach over that area of school life. Because of the bond you share with your students, you at first be the only one to be able to see that talent in that child. But when you get her the specialized training she needs and that talent blossoms into a wonderful skill that can bless others and the child's life as well, you will have given her a gift for life.

Going to bat for your students also means not throwing any children away. When young people are put into your care, that is a serious commitment that you are making to those children. There is not one single child in your care of lesser value than the others. So one way you demonstrate your commitment to being a teacher to every child is when one of your students gets in trouble you go to him or her and find a way to save that child's educational career.

The last thing you want to see is a child expelled and sent out into the world with the stigma of "not good enough" for school. You have it in your power to get that child into alternative schools, to get him or her tutoring until this rough patch passes or to get him or her moved into a home school situation so the many years of education for that youngster

^^^

are not lost over a difficult time in the life of the child.

The place you are granted in the life of your students is one of trust and caring that is a privileged one indeed. Be sure you protect and cherish that gift by going to bat for your students when they need you there. And who knows, down the road your students may come back and go to bat for you in some way when you really need them too.

Good Reasons to Teach

The teaching profession is a unique career field in a lot of ways. Because you are taking on the challenge of educating children or teenagers, along way you will become very much a part of their society with the entire positive and negatives that go with that. It's for that reason that before you make even the first step toward making teaching your career, it's good to examine your motivations to make sure you have good reasons to teach.

The downsides of teaching are well known. Teaching historically does not pay well, particularly if you teach at the public school level. You can find niche situations that pay well like working for a wealthy private school, tutoring or working for a "for profit" teaching operation. But by and large, you don't go into teaching for the money.

∧∧∧

That said it is also true that if you are a good teacher and your resume is strong, you can expect strong job security. There is always a need for good teachers. Unlike going into business, you do not have to make your employer profitable to be a success teaching. You are judged in lives and in the results of your teaching that is evidenced in the grades and strong academics of your students. If you can learn to teach young minds and bring them wisdom and knowledge, you will have a job for life.

    Many people go into teaching because they love the academic environment. For those who grieved the closing of each school year and who never wanted to leave high school and then college, teaching lets you take up residence in that part of society that fits your personality so well. To those who have no idea how the calling to teach works, this seems insane because for many getting out of school a stronger motivation than continuing on in the academic world. So if you have an affinity for the social setting of a school system and the idea of taking up residence in a culture that the pursuit of knowledge is, at least in theory, the primary goal of the institution, teaching is for you.

  Another motivation many have for going into teaching is love of your subject matter. If you have always been passionate about mathematics, history, philosophy, art or physical education, one way to feel fulfillment of your passion is to pass along not only your knowledge about your field of expertise but your passion as well. This is particularly true of a field of study where there is no direct corollary in the business world such as history or philosophy. By making a career in academics teaching the fields of knowledge you love and excel at, you keep the legitimacy of that area of knowledge alive by passing it along to the next generation.

If the core reason you love to teach is the love of your subject matter, you do have to be a realist especially if you find yourself teaching in the public schools. Don't go into a classroom of 30 high scholars and expect every one of them to become a zealot about your field of expertise as you are. Yes, from time to time you will light a fire under a kindred spirit and see the light come on about the love of your subject area.
That experience alone can make the sacrifices of teaching worth it. But be reconciled that if all you do

is at least hold the attention of the students and broaden their knowledge and appreciation of your field of knowledge, for many that is all you can expect. But you are still an educator and you have done a good thing at even that very basic level.

Teaching is a calling no matter what your core reasons to teach is. A true teacher does not go into the field for the money or for a glamorous or exciting career. The excitement of teaching is seeing young minds come alive in class and to take youth people one step further along their path to becoming truly educated individuals. And if that is your passion and what gets you out of bed each morning to go to that school and deal with the negatives of a teaching day, then you have found the right reasons to teach which means you will be successful, well liked and remembered by your students as a great teacher.

∧∧∧

I Want to Teach in Your School

A job interview to teach in a public school or in any institution of learning for children or youth is unlike any other kind of job interview. And it is worth our time to discuss what makes that kind of job interview so different so you can go in and land that job you want and get the next step of your career in teaching well on the way.

In a job interview for a teaching position, two things dominate the discussion. The first one is the regular interview stuff such as your résumé, your background, your education, any publishing history you have and your job history. So to quickly get that part of the interview in order, bring a well prepared resume with you. Now when preparing your resume, keep in mind that the resume does not get you the job. The resume gets you in the door for the interview and serves as a skeleton outline of which you are so the school and the administrator interviewing you knows that at a basic level, you have the credentials to be a good teacher at their school.

It is the second aspect of a job interview for a teaching position that will make the difference between whether you will be hired or not. And that is how the interviewer does when he or she envisions you teaching in one of the classrooms in their building. During the interview, the questions that are asked and the way the interviewer looks at you tells you that he or she is picturing you teaching the students in their school and how you represent yourself as well as your demeanor and personality are what will give that administrator a good feel for your teaching style as well.

^^^

NOT JUST A TEACHER

So customize everything about your interview presentation around looking and acting like the kind of teacher this administrator wants in his or her school. You can start with your outfit. Don't dress so formally that you bring the appearance of a harsh school masquerade. Look at the actual wardrobe you will wear when you are teaching a class of this new boss. Pick out something visually pleasing, relaxed and yet professional so the administrator feels that you would be a warm and yet efficient personality to influence young minds in their school.

In an interview setting, we often worry about what we will say in response to questions. But what will be the determining factor in whether you land the teaching position is not what is said verbally but what you communicate with your facial expressions, the way you express your ideas and the enthusiasm you bring to the interview. These are subtle nonverbal elements of your interview demeanor that the interviewer may not even know are influencing the decisions of who to hire. But they are powerful massages that can really only be communicated through inflection, genuine interest in the interview process and personality.

There are a number of questions the interviewer is trying to get answers to that he or she can never really ask out loud. But these questions are very much a part of this interview and the extent to which you answer these questions correctly will make all the difference when the hiring decision is made. Some of the questions include…

- Does this person love children?
- Does this person have a passion for teaching?
- Will this person fit in with the culture of our school?
- Will the students enjoy this new teacher?
- Is this teacher even tempered and able to handle crisis?
- Will this teacher comply with our policies and procedures?
- Is this teacher a creative person?
- Will this teacher stay with us for a long time so

> I don't have to do this interview again?

All of these questions can be answered in the way you present yourself, in your smile, your laugh and your ability to relax during the interview. The kinds of stories from our past and how you tell those stories will surface that you really do love to teach and you are the kind of teacher who bonds naturally with students and brings out the best in them. And if you can get that message across during the interview, you will land the job every time.

∧∧∧

Meeting the Class for the First Time

P reparing to become a teacher is a big undertaking. It's easy to get caught up in getting through college with a degree in teaching, passing your teachers certification examination
, finding the kind of teaching position you want and getting through the interview that there is one more level of challenge that awaits you that you may not have put some thought into. That is the moment you walk into a classroom and face that sea of little faces looking up at you fearfully and you realize, perhaps with some terror that you really are a teacher and these students expect you to do the job.

Every teacher has a priority for what will happen in that first encounter with the class of students. For some teachers, it's important to establish your authority and to let the kids know you are boss and they will be called up on top live up to your expectations. For another, the first goal in that first hour is to just get organized. But it's a great idea to think through exactly how you are going to handle that first meeting so you establish a relationship with these kids that will result in a very productive and yet happy and peaceful class time experience each day.

As you look at those eyes staring at you, what do you suppose they are thinking? Well, it isn't really that much of a mystery. They are very curious about their new teacher and the things they want to know about you are not things they will ask you out loud including…

∧∧∧

NOT JUST A TEACHER

- ➤ Is this new teacher mean or nice?
- ➤ Will she make us work harder than our last teacher?
- ➤ Is the new teacher funny or too serious?
- ➤ Will she make us move our chairs
- ➤ Is this new teacher boring?

That last question is probably the one that weighs on the minds of most students the most. To a young mind the one crime that should be punishable by death is for you to be boring. They are also wondering what will be the first thing you will say to them to get the relationship started. They are very curious about you as a person and if you will make learning fun or, again that terrible word, "boring".

It is a great idea if you take the time to think out in advance exactly what you want to accomplish in this initial meeting with your new class. One suggestion that has some real value is to seek to find a way to move from strangers to friends fairly quickly and to communicate to the students that you want to work with them as a team. If you and your students become one unit with the shared goal of learning what they have to learn to get good grades to take home to mom and dad and to do so without being "boring", you will have created an educational setting that will be rich with learning potential.

One way to get that relationship off and running in great shape is to do something unexpected when you address them initially. Tell a joke, introduce yourself with a funny illustration from your childhood or in some other way surprise your new class in a fun and lighthearted way. This communicates to them that you are going to be a fun teacher and that they need to come to class paying attention because they never know what to expect. With that kind of rapport, you will have established a relationship that will only continue to open up and grow more trusting and more productive. And it all started because you refused to be that one thing that students hate. You refused to be **"boring"**.

Passing the Teacher's Certification Test

Most of us learn a lot about how to take exams when we are in university or college. But the day you go to take your test to gain your teacher's certification which will give you the license to teach anywhere in the world can be a day of significant stress. The more you can do to prepare for that test will go a long way to help you keep your nervousness down and survive the testing environment in good shape.

Along with good preparation habits that tap all of the many resources available to you to be ready for this important test, you must have a strategy for taking the test itself. You may recall in college that you may have had a series of superstitions as well as test taking habits that helped you face big tests and survive finals week. In the same way when you walk into that testing facility to take and pass your Teacher's Certification Test, a strategy for taking the test can be just as important as your preparation strategy that you

∧∧∧

used to get ready for this important day.

Probably the biggest enemy you will face on testing day is nervousness. Because of the importance of the day and the pressure of the testing environment, anxiety and the testing jitters can become extreme enough to rob you of your concentration and make it less possible for you to focus and do well on the test. So anything we can do to reduce or eliminate test jitters is a big benefit to you when the testing time is upon you.

The preparation process is very much part of your test taking strategy. That is because if you have taken advantage of every coaching and reviewing process, done your remedial study and taken practice exams until they were virtually memorized, you can walk into that testing facility fully confident that you will do well. When you take away any potential for surprises and everything you will encounter in that testing situation is well known and understood, the test day goes from being a day of stress to a day of preliminary celebration because you are that ready to take the certification test.

      Before going into the testing hall, make sure you are well rested and well fed. Don't take any chances with the meals you have before the test. Be sure you eat foods that will settle in your digestive system well and that will give you the energy you need to get through the testing process well. If you do have any spiritual, superstitious items or rituals you feel you must do, do them. This is no time to go through repentance for your superstitious ways. Anything that you can do to relax and be ready to take that test you should do.

    Be aware of what you can bring into the test with you both to take the test and in terms of items for your comfort. If you will be able to take the test better with mints or gum at hand, bring those in. Be sure you have had your trip to the lavatory and that your clothing is loose and comfortable on your body. In every way possible eliminate any physical distractions that will cause you worry or anxiety or distraction from the task at hand of passing this important test so you can start your career as a teacher.

    When the test gets underway, be methodical and complete in your process of working through the test.

First read the test carefully and slowly. Make sure you are absolutely sure you understand everything about the instructions so you can follow them to the letter. The Teacher's Certification Test is timed so use your time well but don't let that clock keep you from moving forward in a steady but patient fashion. Keeping your head under pressure will help you finish the test in good time and do well on marking your answers as well.

      Go through the test and answer the questions that are easy first. This will increase your confidence when you see that you have finished 60% of the test easily and quickly. Then when you see you have the majority of the time left for the few remaining questions, you can take your time and reason them out. This approach to testing along with careful marking of your answers is a proven method to assure your success.

∧∧∧

So What Do You Want to Teach?

When a person introduces themselves to you as a teacher, the question that you invariably ask is "So what do you teach?" How the person answers that question can tell you a lot not only about how they feel about their calling as a teacher and how they feel about their students as well. Usually you get one of two answers. Either the answer is "Oh I teach junior class" or "I teach Algebra". If the answer is a grade level, the teacher probably handles more than one topic. If the answer is a topic such as algebra, then the teacher is a specialist in that topic bringing that area of knowledge to any gathering of students who are assigned to his or her room.

If you are thinking about becoming a teacher, you might pose the question to yourself of, "So what do you want to teach?" It's a question that is loaded with meaning. Because how you answer that question may determine if you are a person who has a passion for a particular topic that is looking for an audience, any audience, to listen to it being taught or if you are a true teacher. Because if you ask a true teacher what they want to teach, the answer will come back, "I want to teach students."

That analysis may seem a bit snobby but the distinction is an important one. The distinction will tell the tale about how well that teacher will relate to his or her students and how long that such a teacher will last in an academic setting. You can tell when you have met a subject based teacher. They only speak with passion about the topic. They have an absolute fascination which may border on an obsession with the topic area. And they have very little tolerance for anyone who does not share that passion for the topic.

So is that person a teacher? Well in the most general sense of the word, yes he or she is because they do have the job of passing their specialized knowledge along to a student group. But it might be more apt to call such a teacher a lecturer or a recruiter because their real devotion is to the topic, not to the students. A subject based teacher is impatient with students who either are not showing talent and passion for their topic area or who interrupt their subject based monologue with questions which only break his stream of thought.

The root word of the term "teacher" is "teach". The definition of teaching then is to build knowledge and skills in a student. You may have found the use of the term we used "a true teacher" a bit elitist. But a teacher who is in the career field of teaching because they have an unquenchable passion for seeing students become educated and who takes delight from seeing students "light up" when they "get it" is indeed a true teacher.

A true teacher is far less obsessed with a perfect discussion and dialog about the topic at hand as they are obsessed with taking a body of young people and turning them from a random gathering of kids into "students". A true teacher is as much concerned with inspiring a desire to learn as he or she is with the topic being taught. And for a true teacher, the student's experience is more important the outline of the day and if

^^^

they can take an hour and turn a disinterested youth into a passionate student of learning, that is an hour well spent.

I went through this exercise so you can apply some of these criteria to your own desire to become a teacher. Examine your motivations. If you are going into teaching to make converts to your love of your subject area, you will do some good no doubt. But because you will encounter frustrations and meet students who will never share you love of your topic, the danger of burn out is high and the possibility of a long career in teaching is low.

Be a "true teacher" and seek the good of your students. And if you go into the work to create students from disinterested young people, you are in the right line of work and will enjoy a long and rewarding career in teaching.

Talking to Students or talking AT them

There is a phenomenon that all public speakers encounter when they are addressing a crowd that if you thought about it very much, it would get to you. It is a phenomenon that any teacher who is trying to impart knowledge to a room full of students will experience as well. And if you think about it very much, it will get to you too. That phenomenon happens when you are talking along and you look out at those blank faces staring up at you and you realize that a few, some or maybe all of those minds behind those faces are paying absolutely no attention to you at all.

Whether or not that drives you crazy depends on whether you consider the act of teaching complete when you speak or when the student grasps and understands what you are saying. Very often when you see a teacher speaking you know that this teacher has absolutely no concern for whether the students are getting it or not. They do not consider it their job to make sure the students understand or interact with the lesson. They are a delivery vehicle and if they vocalize the lecture successfully, they have successfully "taught".

But just saying words into the air whether or not they are heard or understood really isn't teaching, is it? Put it in the context of a chef. If you cook a wonderful meal that is delicious, prepare it with the finest of materials and present it with perfect ambiance, is it still a delightful meal if there is nobody at the table to appreciate it and nobody eats the meal? No, you are only a chef when the patron dines on your food and appreciates every nuance of the flavor

∧∧∧

NOT JUST A TEACHER

and the experience of enjoying what you have done.

That distinction is what drives teachers crazy when they feel students are not listening. To a teacher who has a passion for the real act of teaching, their job is not done until the students grasp the material and interact with it, question it and finally grasp it and make that knowledge their own. A lecture not heard, not understood, not "taught" is not teaching at all, it's just talking.

Preparing to become a teacher is about more than just knowing how to design a lesson plan and how to organize a class room and make a bulletin board. Becoming a teacher means you become one of those amazing people who can take students from uninformed to informed and from unenlightened to truly "taught". When it is your calling to become that kind of teacher to just talk at students with no knowledge of whether they know what you are saying at all is absolutely unacceptable.

This means that you will have to change your teaching style. It means that you won't be satisfied with just working through a lecture. In fact, it might spell the end of the lecture as a teaching device for you entirely. To really find out if those kids are listening and interacting with the material, you will have to change your approach to an interactive teaching style. You will have to start talking to students or with students and not AT them. But once you do that, the feedback you will get and the quality of your teaching will improve so dramatically, you will never want to go back.

∧∧∧

Test Driving a Teaching Career

Deciding to become a full time teacher is a big step. You may be able to remember teachers from your youth that seemed to make it look easy and fun to be a teacher. So if you think you might have the temperament for teaching and that it would be a rewarding career, the best way to find out more about it is to test drive being a teacher in various limited settings to get an idea for how it feels to be a teacher before you launch into the career full time.

The first thing you want to get exposure to is how it will feel to stand in front of a room full of children or young people to present a lesson to them. If you have never done it, it can be a terrifying moment. It is similar to public speaking with the added twist that young people can be fidgety, might be prone to shout things out without notice and can misbehave right in the middle of your presentation which is not something you see that often when doing a presentation to adults.

There are lots of volunteer situations where you can test drive speaking to groups of youngsters to see if it is something you want to do every day. You can volunteer to read to children at the local library or teach Sunday School at your church and have that responsibility for an hour and then it is over. Now, don't be too concerned if you are terrified the first time you look out at that sea of little faces. That is so common it would be surprising if you didn't. Lots of full time teachers with years of experience still get that terror when they open their class each morning.

^^^

NOT JUST A TEACHER

But if you get through the session and have an exhilaration and that feeling that even though it was scary, you want to get in front of them again, you may have the stuff of a teacher inside you trying to get out. And you can get a long term assignment in a volunteer role to "scratch that itch" to teach young people until you finally make the jump to a full time career in teaching.

But there is more to teaching than just talking in front of a class. To really understand how a day of a teacher goes, look for an opportunity to volunteer to be a teacher's aid from time to time. If you can sit in on a class for a day and help out every so often, you can see how a day in the life of a real teacher works. You can witness how the lesson plan is put together and how the preparation of the teacher makes it possible for her to move from lesson to lesson smoothly without losing the attention of the students.

Being in an actual working classroom is the best possible situation for either getting hooked on becoming a teacher yourself or find yourself running in terror for the door. Either way, you will know for sure if you have the "stuff" for the job of teaching. During a classroom day, there will be disruptions that naturally occur. You can learn from a seasoned professional how to smoothly handle them so they do not disrupt the teaching environment You can see how that teacher handles discipline issues, group projects and moves the children from small group sessions, to individual study times and then back to general class participation with easy and skill. These are all skills for you to conquer and seeing them in action is the best way to learn them.

^^^

NOT JUST A TEACHER

The next step from there is to become a full fledged substitute teacher. Now work with your local school districts because you may have to have some training and certification to be able to substitute teaches. But by being available and ready to step in for a teacher, who is ill or called away, you will suddenly have an entire classroom of children for you to teach and you can test drive running a full day of activities in the classroom.

Naturally it won't go perfectly at first. But you can stay at each of these phases until you feel comfortable to move on. And when you conquer that stage of orientation to teaching, you can take that final step and become a full time teacher yourself.

The Brass Tacks About Teaching

Like any job, teaching children is often idealized and romanticized by young people preparing for a career in education. Then once the reality of what life is like as a teacher hits, it can come as a rude shock. This does not mean that the ideals and values of teaching the next generation of youth and the great thrill of seeing a young mind come alive with knowledge are not wonderful and worthy of respect and praise. In truth, anyone who makes it in the field of teaching must have that idealism that is a deep part of your motivation system because it will be those values that will help you get past the hard times that teaching, particularly in a public school situation often brings with a job of teacher.

But along with the values and ideals, we need to mix that inner drive with a strong dose of reality so that when you show up for your first day and work through your first year of teaching, you are not broadsided by some of the challenges and frustrations that lie ahead. A few moments talking about the brass tacks of a teaching career can help you prepare for the negatives so they are less potent and less able to stop you from being a success in your teaching career.

Probably one of the areas of teaching that often causes high teacher stress and burn out is the level of government regulation and the extent that the administration of a school gets in the way of the teaching process. Many times in public school it almost seems like education is of a lesser value than paying attention to rules and regulations and maintaining order and discipline in the school.

When you come to that teaching position with priority placed on teaching students the subject matter at hand and see them begin to excel academically and you find academics taking a back seat to the schools administrative issues, to discipline issues and to what seems to be a nonstop flood of forms and requirements for every governmental program imaginable, that can cause frustration about the job you have taken in that school.

Under funding of education probably ranks second greatest frustration with the working world of teaching. This lack of funding is evident in your pay and in how well the classes you need to teach are funded. You may not have the supplies you need and many teachers actually find themselves buying supplies from their own money just to make sure their teaching is successful. That is the contrast between the public's lack of substantial support for education and your deep commitment to it. But the funding issue can also result in overcrowding of classrooms because the school cannot afford more classrooms or sufficient number of teachers to handle a high student population.

The third problem that often broadsides new teachers is that many students are not the angels we wish they would be. Especially in a public school setting, you will have in every class some students who don't care about academics and would rather disrupt the class than allow you to teach those who do want to learn. It takes some real experience and some coaching from experienced teachers in how to handle this kind of student

∧∧∧

but at least be aware that they will be in your classroom day one and all year long.

It takes some innovative thinking and almost stubborn insistence on staying positive to be a successful teacher under circumstances like this. But if you keep your focus on the kids and on those moments that do come in each school year when you really connect with students and you see them get excited about what you are sharing, that one moment makes dealing with all of the other frustrations entirely worth it.

The Costume of a Teacher

One of the bibles of the business world is a book called **"Dress for Success."** This book describes how to dress for the roll of a successful business person and that wardrobe will help you step into that role. In many ways the "Dress for Success", tells us that how we dress for work is somewhat our "costume" and that putting on that costume of a business professional, you naturally begin to play that role.

Most schools will have a dress code that you will have to abide by as a teacher much as they do for the students. That dress code assures that you will dress in a way that is not dangerous or districting or inappropriate to the job of teaching. And that dress code brings you in line with what the administration expects of the students. But aside from those general guidelines, there is a lot of leverage left to you in your dress so you can express your personality in the "costume" you wear to teach students.

The important thing to remember about the outfits you select is that they do send a message to the students. If you dress very formally, you are telling them to address you respectfully and that you are very much the adult here and they are not. Even if students don't know they are getting your message, they are and even you don't know you are sending a message, you are. So it's a good idea to think about what message your outfits are sending and how you might customize your wardrobe so the students understand who you are and what your expectations are of them just from how you present yourself to them in class.

One big message to send with your costume is, **"I am the teacher and you are the students here."** This is not a message of superiority. It is a message of distance. First of all, be aware that this distance between you and the student socially is necessary and must be part of your approach to your job if you want to be successful in a long term. The classroom is no place for a midlife crisis. Even if you like dressing in a stylish or youthful way outside of class, in class, dress like an adult and in a formal enough way that your clothing makes a clear demarcation between you and them.

This distinction actually makes your students feel more at ease with you. Students get uncomfortable when the adults over them try to blend in to youth culture too much and become "with it". Youth people like the authority figures in their lives to be clearly designated and for you to live up to your role as authority figure in your behavior, your language and your wardrobe. So "dress for success" by having your clothing say, I am the teacher and the students will respond in kind.

Your outfits also have to be practical. Sometimes teaching can become a physical event. You must be prepared to bend down to pick things up and to do some level of low key physical labor even with students in the classroom. This means no tight clothing that restricts your range of motion. It means no short skirts that have you worried about the hemline and your legs all day long and shoes that can keep you going for an entire day of very a very active teaching life.

Just as almost every profession has guidelines for how to dress, these hidden messages and quiet efficiencies you include in your wardrobe selection will go a long way toward making your teaching day successful and comfortable. When your wardrobe is right and you are dressing in the costume of a teacher, you will "become" a teacher and step into that role you were born to play.

∧∧∧

The Courage of a Teacher

When you think of career fields that call for courage, jobs that may call for loss of life are most often thought of. So the career fields of firemen, policemen or the military are jobs that involve a great deal of courage that we cannot discount. Teachers, by contract don't really think of themselves as strong or brave individuals compared to these more obvious choices. But it takes a tremendous courage to be a teacher in ways that it is worthwhile to acknowledge as we are doing here today.

The courage of a teacher goes beyond just being willing to stand up in front of 20-30 wiggly children every day and try to guide them through their studies. Of course, standing up in front of that kind of crowd does take a lot of guts. Children are notoriously unpredictable crowd. And while the chances you will see physical harm speaking to a classroom of youngsters are small, it is a public speaking nightmare and facing that kind of nightmare takes a real courage not many needs on a daily basis.

Going into teaching as a lifestyle choice is also a courageous decision. Teaching is well known to be both a low paying position and one that affords little thanks to the teacher. Teachers are often the target of attacks by parents all the while they are enduring considerable sacrifices just for the privilege of teaching young people. Many times budgets for schools are cut so that class sizes swell and a teacher who wants nothing more than to be able to mentor and love a small group of children finds a class room of twice

^^^

that size put before him or her to teach. Or the supplies budget for schools gets slashed so many times teachers will go out with their own money and buy the classroom supplies they need so the young can be educated and the classroom can function despite these problems.

There is an emotional risk that teachers openly embrace every year they take on a new class. A lot more goes on between a teacher and a class of students as that teacher puts out instruction to make those children better people. A bond and a love develop that is valuable to the educational process. This affection often carries on into childhood for the children who will speak with fondness of that favorite teacher decades ago.

But for the teacher, as soon as that bond becomes mature at the end of a year of teaching, those children move on and they must prepare their hearts for a new set of kids in the fall. That emotional roller coaster is a wrenching experience that teachers embrace to be able to continue doing the one thing they love to do which is to teach.

This is not to say that there are no physical dangers or acts of heroism that teachers often exhibit when the need arises. In any urban schools, courageous teachers face injury or worse from students who are **gang members** who threaten them with dire injuries for being there to do the one thing they are called to do which is to teach. Further, we have documented cases where school shootings put students in danger that teachers put themselves in harm's way and even lost their lives to protect their students. We see this in our society today and at other crisis situations as well. And that kind of willingness to become a martyr to save a student is a classic example of what it means to be courageous.

    As you prepare your career path toward becoming a professional teacher, you may not have ever thought of yourself as courageous. But because of the sacrifices you are about to make and because the only real reward of being a teacher is the joy of imparting knowledge to young students, there is a nobility to what you are about to do that is worthy of recognition and honor. And while society will not necessarily take the time to give honor to the courage of teachers, it's a good thing when we do that so it is documented here that teachers are truly a courageous lot and we can all be glad for their influence on our children's lives and on society in general.

The Cyber Teacher

Becoming a teacher today is means learning to teach with new tools and resources that were unheard of only twenty years ago. There is almost no part of the education experience that is untouched by the computer or the internet. So the more you look to becoming a "cyber teacher", the more you will be tapping the great power cyberspace has given us to use for education.

A cyber teacher doesn't mean that you will no longer interact with your students in class. "Going cyber" means that you will take advantage of the internet even during the course of a teaching day to tap the incredible information resources that are there to make your lessons so much more rich and meaningful.

It is almost unheard of any more for a class room to not be equipped with not one but many internet connections and computers as well as all of the popular software to support the use of computers in the classroom. In fact, more and more students are bringing laptops with wireless internet access to use at their desks which means that the computer is now becoming as common a student tool as the pencil or the protractor for your students.

Staying up to date with the latest that is available on the internet is critical so you are offering your students the best teaching available in this modern time. Moreover, you have to stay up to date and "plugged in" to what is going on in cyberspace because your students are knowledgeable about what is happening in the internet world. So to

∧∧∧

stay up with them, you have to stay current too.

Along with in class research resources, the internet has set up tools for communication that were unheard of before. When you assign group projects, they won't just communicate by sitting around a table and working out the project. They can interact via internet "groupware" such as facebook groups, twitter, whatsap, wikis or Google groups to share information, pool their resources and even split up the work to be done which all can be easily merged into their final project report to turn in to you when they are done.

This new age of communication can be used by you as

a teacher to open up communications channels with the students at home and with their parents in ways never known before as well. No longer do you have to worry about laboriously writing out the daily assignments for your students to write down and take home. You can now post them to a class online bullion board or email them to the parents and to the student so every day when the child gets home, the excuse that "I lost my homework assignment" just won't cut it.

To make this work, you also have to make sure the parents are internet savvy. Don't count on the child to give his or her mom and dad a seminar in cyber education because the speed of cyberspace makes the student life more accountable. But you can schedule computer classes with the parents to show them how to find the student's assignments as well as grades, notes from the teacher or special announcements right here on the class web page in cyberspace.

^^^

NOT JUST A TEACHER

We are really just getting started tapping the internet to make communications and education more efficient and powerful. Other ways to use this technology includes having the students do their homework online so they cannot say "the dog ate my homework." And because young people are very internet savvy, by making their education life internet enabled, they will be better students. And you will be a better teacher because you took the time to learn to tap the power of the internet to become a cyber teacher for your students as well.

The Inner Calling to Teach

When you determine that you want to be a teacher of children or teenagers, that is much more than a career decision. It is a commitment to the future generation and an expression of nobility in you that would not be seen in any other way. Unlike many other lines of work, people go into teaching for other reasons than just an interest in the career field or a way to make a paycheck.

It's sometimes difficult to put into words what your motivations are that drive you to pick teaching as your career. This is especially true if you are asked by friends why you made that choice. In many ways teaching is misunderstood and if you voiced what that inner calling to teach feels like, that urge to educate the young takes on the trappings of the calling of a missionary or a martyr. So you probably don't voice your real motivations because they might sound

∧∧∧

corny to someone who is not carrying that special calling as you are.

    Part of that urge to teach the young is a bond between you and the next coming up generation that makes you driven to offer your talents, your education and your life to teach the young important information and to model life skills for them as well. That bond with the very young may have originated in you when you were a child yourself. But for a teacher who is called to the profession at a very deep level, that calling does not go away which is why so many teachers stay with the job decade after decade only willing to lay it down when health issues brought on by age forces the issues.

But the teaching calling is not entirely altruistic. There are some real rewards that also exist on the emotional and ethical level to being a teacher. Just seeing young people respond to knowledge and to your leadership as their teacher is deeply gratifying to one who is called to this profession. And when you are teaching a classroom of 20-30 kids, that gratification can become magnified many times over. It is a great experience of excitement when you see so many children do well and move on to their next grade all because of what you offered to them as their teacher.

Teaching young people is also a tremendous amount of fun. Yes, as their teacher it is your task to keep them on task to complete their lessons and keep moving toward their goal of finishing their educational objectives of the day and of the year. But along the way you become a friend of the child and the child a friend of yours. There are literally scores of moments of the sheer joy of play between

^^^

teacher and student that is grounded in a pure form of friendship that is a hidden benefit to committing to a classroom of children to teach and mentor them to success.

The calling to teach is one that is buried deep in the soul of the teacher and for many, it goes unfulfilled. The difficulties of teaching or the rigorous training that society requires of teachers often keeps away many talented teachers who cannot make those kind of sacrifices. But for those that can, the sense of fulfillment of a mission and the pride and satisfaction of seeing your students do well is a reward for teaching that is impossible to describe and impossible to replace as well.

The Power of Differentiation

The last few chapters have taught us a great deal about how students work and think and the differences between different students and how those differences change the way those students process information and learn. On the surface, as a teacher, it's easy to say, well I cannot change my curriculum to suit every possible learning disability or quirk of personality. That is the old model of teaching that has been in place for many decades. Students came to a centralized class and the way the lessons were presented was what they got and it was up to the student to adjust to be successful or a failure.

The problem with that model is that it puts the weight of the responsibility to be successful in education on the student. That is all well and good at the college level where the students are essentially adults and they are expected to be ready to bare a larger level of responsibility. But at the elementary level, the burden of assuring that the student not only hears the lesson but understands it lies with the teacher. So in the last few years, a teaching style called **"differentiation"** has come along that utilizes innovative classroom methods to help all students come away with a solid understanding of the material, not just the few who were able to adjust to the single approach the teaching of the old model.

Differentiation begs the question, "Who is responsible for the education of the children?" The system where the children were exposed to a lecture, given an assignment which may have been cryptic to understand and sent home for the hapless portents to understand what was expected is at best ineffective and at worst just plain lazy.

Modern approaches to education see the job of the teacher as not just to present information and to correct papers. The job of the teacher is to teach and that teacher is not a success until every student in his or her class has learned the information well and can interact with it to demonstrate that the information has become knowledge which is useful and applicable in daily life. This is a high requirement on teachers but anything short skirts the objectives of the teaching profession entirely.

One difference between students that drastically effects how well the student learns is learning styles. Some students are visual learners meaning they do well when they learn by seeing. Others can absorb and process information audibly whereas others must physically interact with the material to truly grasp it. Differentiation changes the way class time is used so the same information is presented in a variety of teaching methods so all students can use each style to fully grasp the material.

Differentiation may not have been possible before we had so many new teaching tools available via the internet. But with online resources, we can tap the power of video online and utilize online activities so that learning is no longer just listen, write it down and repeat it on a test. Learning now is interactive and repetitive in many different ways to the same information is processed uniquely each time. The outcome is the student not only can learn through the learning style that fits his or her personality but that learning is deeper and longer lasting.

Adapting your teaching style to fully tap the power of differentiation will take some time. There are new technologies to learn to use and a new approach to the daily lesson plan to understand and learn to work with. But once you are simultaneously teaching many while addressing the individual learning styles and unique characteristics of each child, you will find the outcome of your teaching so much more effective that you will never want to go back.

^^^

The Social Side of School

If you are preparing to become a teacher with the anticipation of leading a group of 20 or more students into the process of academic discovery, it is easy to let most of your concentration be focused on academics and on focusing that class on the school work at hand. You envision yourself in front of a big group of fascinated youngsters who are all about paying attention to what you have to say.

There is a fallacy in this image though and it lies in what will be actually going in the minds of those students you will try to teach each day. The fundamental flaw in this assumption is that when you are looking out at a group of a couple dozen kids that their minds are only on you because the class is all about you and the topic at hand in your lesson plan. The truth is that the class is all about each other and the social side of any classroom setting can come to totally dominate the classroom time for the kids.

If you do not recognize or don't know how to diagnose what is going on socially in your classroom, you are working at a distinct disadvantage. Kids are learning a lot at school and not all of it is what you have prepared for them to learn. The social setting in that classroom is teaching them all kinds of lessons that you have no control over. Moreover, some of those lessons may not be wholesome or socially acceptable concepts.

The society of children and teenagers can be amazingly brutal. Kids are far more harsh on each other than adults would ever imagine and the harm that can be done to the heart and soul of someone who gets singled out to be victimized can be lifelong and devastating. So it is to your advantage if you learn to recognize the signs of unhealthy social interaction and jump in and change that group behavior before it goes too far. This will take some keen powers of observation on your part, an ability to spot social exchanges happening even as you teach and the psychology to know what is going on.

    The good news is that as the leadership in the class room, you can effect change in how the kids influence each other socially. Because you know that social skills are being learned all the time around you as you teach, you also have the opportunity to create activities and opportunities for discussion that can change that social behavior for the better. You can literally teach those kids to get along and to treat each other in a civil fashion and do so without alarming the kids or losing any teaching time that you need to complete your academic goals.

One great way to begin to move the kids toward positive social models is to move from the traditional "teacher talks to big class" approach to teaching to one that uses small group activity, teamwork and competition to not only make learning a lot more fun but to encourage good social development that will help the kids develop socially as well as academically.

You should not feel that by trying to teach the kids good social skills you are abandoning your core principles as an educator. If you can also teach the kids good social skills while you have them in your class, that time could turn out to be the most valuable thing you have to offer your students. And when you see those positive social values begin to change lives in your young students, you will get a unique form of pride because it was you that made it happen.

Where the Teacher is Mom

There is an army of teachers in this country and around the world that get no pay, do not show up at a classroom and get no recognition for the work they do. But they are doing the job of teaching young minds and getting them through a year of academic work. These are the minions of home school teachers who are quietly doing the job of education of the next generation. And we have learned from studies into home schooling, they are doing a pretty good job because home schooled students often rank high in higher learning preparation examinations.

If you are considering becoming a teacher in the limited scope of home schooling your own children, the task is not as intimidating as it seems. And the potential benefits to your children are great. Public schools are notorious for taking bright young minds and snuffing out that fire for learning that they were born with.

The reason this happens is simple. Public schools are mandated to teach a very large body of kids so because of the volume of kids they must pass through each grade, the emphasis much be on discipline and order and the priority for high quality academics has to slide so that every child can get through.

That is why the focused and specialized environment of a home school situation is perfect for a bright mind such as your child has because you can customize your curriculum to fit your child and to accelerate as fast as they show an aptitude to go. You don't have to put a big emphasis on being in their seat when the bell rings and being in school uniform down to their underwear. There are no bells in home school and they can come to school in their underwear if they want to. As long as they learn, that is the emphasis in a home school environment.

When you set out to becoming a home school teacher, you have a huge amount of flexibility in how you structure the learning environment. If you have a room you can set aside as the "classroom", that is a nice set up because you and your child know that when you go into that room, learning will happen here. But because the goal in that room is to complete one step along the way to finishing a curriculum, your young student knows that class will be over when they achieve their goals, not when the bell rings and that encourages productivity and focus.

It is also a myth that home schooling will become expensive. In fact, you can virtually set up a perfectly valid year long curriculum for very little cost. By logging into the public school's system, you can find the curriculum for the grade your child is in school and what must be learned to finish that grade. In many cases, local public schools and many private schools have programs to help you get started so that your child follows a similar educational path that is going on down the street in the public schools. This is an advantage to you and the school because should you decide to send your child back to public school the next year, they are not out of step with the program.

Materials can often be had for very little expense as well. Many times a textbook that is being used for a particular subject will come out with a new edition. When that happens, you can pick up copies of the previous edition, now out of date to the public schools, for very little. The topics in the text book are just as valid in the previous edition so you can conduct full year of classes using that textbook and not face any serious cost investment at all.

By looking for ways to take advantage of public facilities like the computers at the public library and of programs offered by churches, public schools and other institutions to help home school teachers like you be successful, you can set up a program at home that will help your child succeed as a student in this educational setting. It will be an adventure for you. And you will see a new appreciation come in to your child's eyes when he or she suddenly realizes that mom is still mom but she is also an outstanding teacher as well.

^^^

NOT JUST A TEACHER

AUTHOR

I.U. Thaddeus is a minister of the word. He is saddled with a mandate of building LEADERS through the teaching of the word. The author has written several books for the benefit of mankind

Entrepreneur, Professional Speaker & Author.

THE MAKING OF A HIGHLY SUCCESSFUL TEACHER

Thaddeus's goal is to help you achieve your personal, career and business goals faster and easier than you ever imagined.

He speaks to corporate and public audiences on the subjects of Personal and Professional Development. His exciting talks, articles and seminars on Leadership, Selling, Self-Esteem, Goals, Strategy, Creativity and Success Psychology bring about immediate changes and long-term results.

I.U.Thaddeus is not just a teacher; he is a highly successful teacher

NOT JUST A TEACHER

www.ingramcontent.com/pod-product-compliance
Lightning Source LLC
Chambersburg PA
CBHW020919180526
45163CB00007B/2810